I0437998

THE SOURCE WITHIN
FOR KIDS & TEENS

ZEMÍ

authorHOUSE®

AuthorHouse™
1663 Liberty Drive, Suite 200
Bloomington, IN 47403
www.authorhouse.com
Phone: 1-800-839-8640

First published by AuthorHouse 10/14/2009

ISBN: 978-1-4490-1589-3 (sc)

Library of Congress Control Number: 2009908624

Printed in the United States of America
Bloomington, Indiana

This book is printed on acid-free paper.

For all the children and teenagers

of our Universe

Table of Contents

INTRODUCTION

This is a different kind of book because it talks about a special topic; what I call *The Source Within*. This refers to an Energy or Power that helps us get through tough times in our lives. It's the inner part of us giving us confidence and courage; it's our intuition and determination; it is responsibility; and it is LOVE.

I believe children are not born bad, evil, or mean; those qualities are learned from those around them. Just like you learn whatever language is being spoken, you learn whatever behaviors you see.

This book was written to help you kids and teens return to your Inner, Loving Self. Be aware you already have *The Source Within* because you are born with it. Your *Source Within* has all the answers so listen to your Inner Self, *The Source Within*, as you grow up and you will <u>know</u> what to do. (*Easy - not always; possible - YES!*)

When you are young, you need caring, loving adults in your life to teach you how to get along in life. But sometimes even a good home may not be without problems.

I want you to remember that life is whatever you make of it. It's not "good" or "bad"; life just is. **Life is what <u>you</u> make it** so make it great. Live with LOVE in your heart;

be good to yourself and others; know you are loved; be who you truly are in spite of what others may say or think; always be honest with yourself and others; always do your best, but most of all, have fun being a kid and a teenager! Enjoy your time as a kid <u>and</u> a teenager because before you realize it, those years are gone!

Enjoy life! Live life! Have fun! Laugh a lot!

If you **ever** need someone to talk to or have questions, email me at <u>source4peace@yahoo.com.</u>

Chapter 1

My life as a kid

Nowadays, it seems like you kids don't play outside as much as we used to. You guys watch TV or play video games most of the time so you're not active. There's nothing wrong with that except since you're not moving around, many of you are gaining lots of unhealthy weight and are lazy. The other concern is many of you end up thinking as "negative" or acting as violent as the shows you watch or games you play. Some of you think those shows or games are just like real life, and they're not! In real life when you shoot someone, they really could die and you do go to jail. You also end up hurting a <u>lot</u> of people (yourself, the victim, their family, your family, and friends). Real life is <u>not</u> a game!

Believe it or not, music and images of violence, sex, and hatred (including language and actions) can alter the way you experience life and interact with others. You learn from what you see just like you learn from your parents and those around you. But I wanted to tell you that **<u>you</u> are the <u>only</u> person in control of how you feel and react. <u>You</u> are responsible for <u>your</u> actions and the choices <u>you</u> make in life.**

When you are bombarded with so many "negative" images, you are not in touch with *The Source Within*. You cannot hear *It* and you will act like *It* doesn't exist. Then LOVE will start to fade away. This is why I believe you kids and teens have so many "problems" and feel so alone and depressed.

Too many of you get caught up in these games or shows and forget to go outside and play (to interact with others). When I was a kid, we used to go outside in the morning and not go back in until dark (except to eat or if mom called us in).

With everyone relying more on technology, your family may forget to make time for outdoor activities. Many families think it's easier to buy you a video game so they can get "things" done. Often, your parents don't check its content for violence, sex, or language and have no clue about what you're seeing. Then, they wonder why you seem so angry.

Too many families today don't "find" the time to do things together although I know a few do make time. And that's good!

It's very important to spend time together whether it's outside or inside. Outdoors you could go swimming, walking, boating, hiking, or playing ball games; indoors you could play music, read, or cook a meal together. Doing these activities as a family helps build up trust and strengthens LOVE. This awakens *The Source Within* in everyone.

My point is – BE ACTIVE! Run, jump, spin around until you're dizzy, walk & talk, look up at the clouds, or play in the rain. If you're inside, then draw, read, sing, dance, be silly, talk, be goofy, be silent, or write.

Write some things you would like to do…

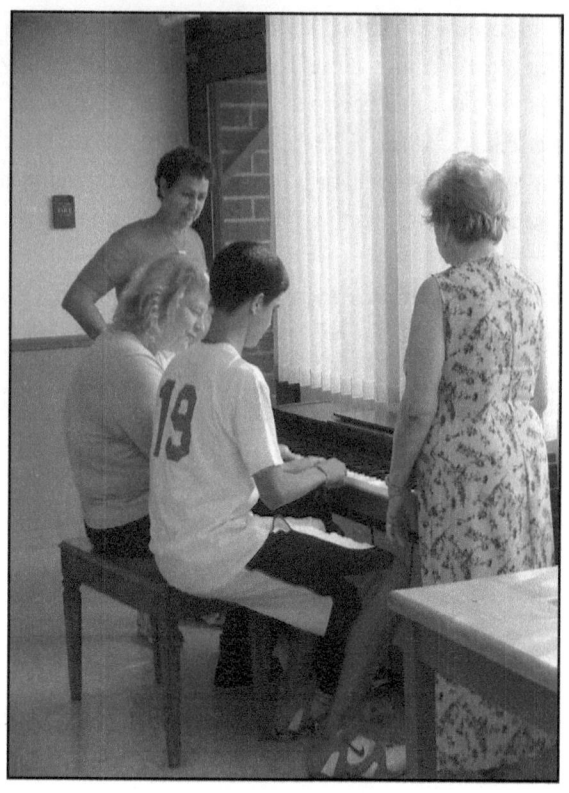

Just have FUN!

Think about this… as you grow up from a baby, you rely on your parents (or some adult) to take care of you and your needs. They <u>are</u> *supposed to* take care of **you** by making sure you have food to eat, a place to sleep so your body can rest, clothes to dress with, and lots and lots of LOVE. These are the essential things you need as a kid. But did you know some kids go hungry because they don't have any food to eat; others do not have clothes to stay warm in the cold; yet others do not have a place to call home to keep them out of harm's way or to be able to sleep?

What would you do if you didn't have these things?

What could you do to help less fortunate kids?

Believe it or not even though there are thousands of kids that don't have some of these essential things, a number of them still grow up healthy and happy.

Why do you think that is?

Well, I think it's because they had Self LOVE. LOVE is part of *The Source Within* you. LOVE heals all wounds. LOVE cannot coexist with hate. You cannot love and hate at the same time. It is impossible! Someone once told me: "If you meet someone you don't like that doesn't mean you have to hate them." That's pretty cool because there will be people you meet that you won't get along with, but it doesn't mean you have to be rude or mean to them; just let them be who they are. If you're LOVED, you will feel and share LOVE with others. LOVE lives within you (and everyone) so find it and keep it strong; don't let it be hidden. Let the *Source* be active in your life!

Many kids today learn the word hate from TV or at home and don't know what it means. They just repeat what they hear! Well, to me it means they do not care if that person, animal, or thing <u>ever</u> existed; that it could be gone from Earth (*you know, not exist*) and it wouldn't matter. That's pretty harsh if you ask me because all living and non-living things on Earth serve a purpose. We are <u>not</u> the ones who should be deciding what things deserve to live and which do not.

We are all born with LOVE in our heart, but we don't hear about it often enough as we grow up. Sadly, many parents do not say "I love you" to their children or hug them. This is why I am teaching you kids and teens to turn to *The Source Within*; to find Self LOVE. <u>Know</u> LOVE lives inside you and you don't have to wait for someone else to give it to you; you already have LOVE inside your own heart!

Now, I want to go back to "family time"... When I was a kid in Puerto Rico we used an old cardboard box to slide down a muddy hill whenever it rained, and we spent lots of time on the beach! We were always together with family and still are! (At least once a year as an entire family.) That's no different than you spending time with your family. You could all take a walk, ride bikes, build a fort, pitch a tent in the backyard, or even work on the yard together. Like I said before, the important thing is being together and spending quality time as a family.

Spending time *with* your family builds trust and encourages LOVE. And that's important! To this day, my family plays games whenever we get together! [This picture was taken last year at my mom's place.]

Another thing we do that many families don't seem to do anymore is sit around the kitchen table and talk about our day, tell jokes, or recount family stories. Many families are different than when I grew up because they *don't seem to* spend much time, if any, together. I hear them say they don't have the time. Well, I say, **"Make time!"** I've seen families eating out, who don't even talk. (*I don't know how*

that is even possible!) I think we all need to learn to have meaningful conversations.

I know texting, cell phones, and email are faster ways to talk, but when you don't spend time <u>in</u> <u>person</u>, you are missing a lot of the LOVE and interaction needed to grow healthy and happy.

What are you willing to do to spend time with your family?

Another issue with many families today is they don't know their neighbors so kids end up home alone. Many of today's families leave their kids and/or teenagers to raise themselves because both parents are working. Kids and teenagers are home without adult supervision, interaction, and LOVE. These children were labeled "latch-key kids".

Write your ideas of how we could help "latch-key kids" not be alone. (Email me your ideas or share them with your parents or teachers.)

While I was growing up, neighbors used to be like family. But nowadays, neighborhood communities don't seem to exist much anymore. That's too bad because neighbors helped each other out and watched (and often fed) each other's kids. It didn't matter to which family you belonged. In reality, neighbors <u>can</u> provide LOVE and safety in your life, too.

My younger sister shared a great idea of how to possibly help rebuild neighborhoods. She said we could create "Community Gardens". So let me explain… to make one, you have to first find a place where everyone can plant together. (It could be one person's yard or a nearby empty lot.) Next, everyone chooses and plants a vegetable, spice, herb, or fruit. They can plant more than one if they want to. *(By the way, seed packets can cost as little as 50 cents.)*

What happens is everyone starts interacting (talking), as they take care of their plants. After the crops grow, each family trades with one another so everyone has plenty of each type of food. So you see, "Community Gardens" help families get acquainted, build trust, and save money from not buying at the market and not driving. Best of all, it brings the neighbors closer together as a "family" and a community. What a great idea, hey!! *(Yeah, my sister is pretty smart!)*

So, what could you do to start a community garden in your neighborhood (or some other activity that would bring everyone together? (Write it down then talk to your parents about it.))

I would like to somehow find a way to help neighborhoods fix old community centers or build community parks where kids can go after school instead of being home alone. Places where there would always be some trusting adult supervision and where kids could interact with other kids.

Doing things together (the human connection) is what builds LOVE. This is what keeps families (and you) connected and strengthens the bond. When you interact with others, you build trust and reinforce LOVE. I believe as long as you share LOVE, you can have a happy family life. I do have to warn you though, even when some families are together life is not "perfect". Sometimes, families don't get along well because LOVE doesn't endure. That's when you (and the family) have to return to *The Source Within*; to find LOVE. The *Source* gives you strength and reassurance (courage) to find LOVE within yourself and one another. (*I believe that's one of the main reasons families have problems – because they forget to find LOVE in each other.*)

To me, "perfection" is an overused word. I say just be the best person you can be <u>and</u> always do your very best because being the *best* you know how to be is perfection at its best! To me, an "A" is not perfection; it is just a letter. So, don't be perfect; **be exceptional; be YOU!**

Write your ideas of what it means for you to be "your best"...

Now, let's talk about a word you will eventually learn and most parents expect teenagers to know about – RESPONSIBILITY. I know this chapter is for kids and not teens, but you might as well start learning about it now!

Responsibility means a few things, like doing your part to help out, telling the truth in every situation, and being respectful. But it means more than that, and you'll learn more about it when you become a teenager.

Sadly, there are some adults who still have not learned responsibility so then their kids don't learn about it. That's why I think some kids are mean or rude to others and don't seem to care. Maybe you can help them learn how to be more responsible and kind by teaching them to find **their** *Source Within.*

Responsibility is doing your part: taking out the trash, making your bed, keeping your room neat, eating the food that is cooked for you, putting away your toys after you play, taking a bath or shower, or even brushing your teeth. These are things you can do to be responsible. When you do your part, it helps out the family and others. Even when you're young, you can learn to pick up after yourself since there's nothing too hard for you to learn or do. You can learn and do just about anything if you decide to! I know kids with disabilities (in a wheel chair) who still do things to help out around the house, like put away their clothes or help clean up. When you do even little things, your parents or adults will appreciate you for it! Besides, think about this… if you do your part to help out and do it without being asked or told then you should have more time to PLAY!

I am sure you had hoped this chapter would not talk about school, but the truth is if you're 5 years old or older then you need this next section.

When you're in school, you <u>will</u> have to do homework; this is work you take home to practice what you've learned at school. It's not supposed to be work for your parents to do <u>for you</u>. You do it to show the teacher what you've learned.

You <u>will</u> learn the things you **understand and pay attention to**. So, while you're in class, pay attention to your teacher! You cannot learn unless you are willing to try and do new things. If you don't do it, you won't find out what you can do! So, do your homework and school work the best way <u>you</u> can. Do it neatly and hand it back in on time! This is part of being responsible.

Now, let's tie this in with *The Source Within… It* can help you learn new things if you don't give up (that's determination). This doesn't mean you will learn everything right away because some things can take longer than others to learn. It's like learning to ride a bike for the first time. Most of us are scared, but something inside of us gives us the COURAGE to do it. That's *The Source Within*! It's the part of you that tells you to do it. It's also the part of you that tells you to get back up on the bike again and again after you fall off.

Well, guess what? That's what learning in school is like, too. You just have to keep on *doing* it until you get it. And believe me – YOU WILL GET IT! Don't allow yourself to get a "bad" attitude toward school or your teachers; even when they don't seem to care just **do <u>your</u> very best**. Teachers and your parents will notice when you are doing your best. It's important to **do things** instead of just trying them; but, it <u>is</u> better to try than not ever try at all. You get it? It is better to <u>**do**</u> things in life! By the way, you could ask questions when you don't understand and get extra help. The important thing to remember is **never give up**!

Ok, now let's talk about parents... Sometimes it may seem like parents don't care, but most do. Just look for the LOVE. Some parents want to raise their kids differently from the way their own parents raised them so they may not discipline you at all. And that can become a problem because you need to know your limits and learn how to be respectful, polite, loving, sincere, and honest with and toward others. So, if your parents don't seem to care, forgive them and LOVE them for doing the best they can.

Other times life can be hurtful because you don't feel loved, your family fights, or someone drinks and hurts you or someone else. These situations can appear hopeless or impossible to get through, but you **can** get through them. Hang on to LOVE (*The Source Within*) and find someone you trust to talk to. There is no shame in asking for help and there's nothing wrong with it because sometimes moms and dads need help, too.

When you are a kid, life can be overwhelming. When you feel like things are getting out of hand (*that's what overwhelming means*), remember that life is not "good" or "bad"; life just is. Life is what you make of it. Depending on how you experience life, you may judge it as good or bad.

Life seems better when unconditional LOVE exists. (Unconditional love is LOVE that doesn't expect anything from you in return; it's just LOVE; it doesn't have conditions with it.) Families are supposed to have unconditional love. Sometimes friends can share unconditional love. Remember *The Source Within* you **is** LOVE and it has no expectations or conditions. Just be yourself and believe in yourself. Remember to talk and spend time with your family and share LOVE. This way, you keep your *Source* active (alive).

Feel free to email me about any of the stuff you wrote about in this chapter: source4peace@yahoo.com I will read it!

CHAPTER 2

WHAT DOES IT ALL MEAN?

I am going to give you more information to make this all a bit clearer for you...

The Source Within

What I mean by *The Source Within* is that you have a special part inside you to help you get through life's tough times. It can help you do things you may otherwise be scared to do. It's a power or energy inside of you (*we all have this*). *The Source Within* makes you feel like you can do anything! It gives you strength, confidence, and courage. The *Source* is LOVE. It's also the part of you that learns to be responsible.

Let's go back to the example of riding a bike...Do you remember the first time your mom or dad took the training wheels off your bike? You weren't sure you were ready, but they wanted you to try it so you did because you trusted them and knew they loved you. You told them, "Ok, but don't let go!" Then they started pushing you along and before you knew it, you were riding all by yourself! That's *The Source Within*. It's the part inside you that allows you to keep riding or says, "You can do it!" (Determination) It is <u>knowing</u> you could do it! (Intuition)

(By the way, if you've never ridden a bike, save some of your money and buy one; it's lots of fun!)

The *Source* is always inside of you. The *Source* does not leave you. You just have to find it and use its power (energy) whenever you face a tough situation. It's like finding the confidence to ride the bike! **Everything is possible with** *The Source Within***; you just have to believe you can do it and do it!**

What's religion got to do with it anyway?

I would like to bring this up because some people will wonder if this has to do with religion. To me, it doesn't; it just has to do with YOU (and me- all of us)! It has to do with finding and relying on our Inner, Loving Self. You don't have to believe in God to know you can do anything, to be courageous or determined, to be responsible, or to feel LOVE. I don't want the idea of religion to keep anyone from reading this book.

Some of you grow up in a home where your family goes to a religious place called church, synagogue, mosque, or temple. If they do, they may say *The Source Within* is called God, Jehovah, Allah, Buddha, Spirit, Goddess, Vishnu, Jesus, or the Christ. *(Sorry, but there are too many names to list them all.)* If they want to name it, they can and that's ok by me. No matter what anyone calls the *Source, it* is the same. It's LOVE!

Some families don't go to any place like that and others don't believe in a Creator (God). That's ok too because we all experience life in our own way from our own point of view; just like you will. None of this thinking is "wrong" because we all have our own perspective *(the way we "see" life)*. You will have your own unique way of learning about life and your own experiences just like everyone on Earth. It may not be the same as your parents, and that's ok, too. The important thing is that you find your way to your Inner, Loving Self *(Source)*. *(We all have The Source Within!)*

A Rabbi once told me it was best to live with the idea of "in addition to" not "instead of". This means we can always learn from other people's points of view or beliefs. We do not have to reject them or their ideas just because they're different than our own. A friend of mine taught me to celebrate our diversity (our differences). That's cool to me because it reminds me of the rainbow. You see, rainbows have to have all of the different colors to be beautiful!

Bottom line is - we all have *The Source Within*. The *Source* is LOVE. The *Source* is inside you so it **is** always with you. The *Source* is the part inside of you that helps you stay out of "negative" or dangerous situations (intuition). It is believing in yourself (confidence) and in your ability to do things by not giving up (determination). All of these attributes exist inside all of us; sometimes we just have to find them. *The Source Within* is <u>knowing</u> you can do anything you put your mind to. No matter how difficult things get in your life as you grow up, you can get through it. Sometimes you may need someone to help you get through it and that's just fine. Rely on *The Source Within* and let LOVE help you get through your life's tough times!

Write what you think *The Source Within* **means.**

CHAPTER 3

MIDDLE SCHOOL - WHAT THE BLEEP?!

Welcome to "teenage-hood"!

I think 13 is an extraordinary age because it's when you start changing from a kid to a teenager *(which I like to call "little adults")*. Did you know in many cultures around the world kids go through a special ceremony to celebrate "coming of age"? Sadly, though, in the United States not too many families believe in this; instead, most adults seem to dread you becoming a teenager. **This should be an amazing time in your life.** Even though you <u>will</u> change physically, mentally and psychologically, you will still be **you** (*The Source*).

By the way, as a teenager you <u>will</u> definitely be expected to become more responsible and mature. I don't know why, but a lot of adults forget what it was like being a teenager. Many of them lost the kid inside of them. So find your *Source* (LOVE) and help them find their inner kid again. If you keep *The Source Within* alive (and active), you won't loose the kid in you when you get older! (*I know because I am just a big kid myself!*)

As a teenager, you are expected to become responsible. You will hear adults talk about responsibility <u>a lot</u>, especially your teachers at middle school.

Do me a favor, before you keep reading, write down what you think "responsibility" means.

Good job! Now, keep reading... As you mature, you need to be responsible for your actions, your obligations (like homework), your role in the family, and for the choices you make. That's a lot to be responsible for! It can get intense because at the same time you're dealing with psychological, physical, and emotional adjustments. Relax though; that's all part of growing up and being a teenager!

So let's talk about "your actions"; these are what your parents and teachers hold you accountable for. For example, these may include being nice or kind to others, not fighting, being respectful, being sincere, dressing suitably, and following school rules. So if your actions are "appropriate", then others will say you are being responsible. If your actions are not, you will not be trusted or you may be yelled at and asked, "Why can't you be more responsible?" So, mind what you say or do.

It's not always easy to be correct with your actions, but you <u>can</u> do it. <u>Here are two suggestions:</u> Think of what could happen if you do or say something a certain way **before** you do it or say it; or, imagine the other person's reaction to what you said or did (*before you say or do it, of course*). If you do this, it might help you avoid misunderstandings and keep you from doing or saying inappropriate things.

But no matter what you do or say, remember <u>you</u> made the choice. For example, in school (*and in life*), you can either follow the rules or not. It <u>is</u> <u>your</u> choice. But with your choices comes responsibility and consequences. The consequence is what happens as a result (after) your action. So let's go back to the above example: If you don't follow the rule of being on time to class then you may serve after-school detention. Part of being responsible would be to accept the outcome (the detention). Remember, **you and only you are accountable for <u>your</u> actions.** Others cannot make you act or feel a certain way. No one else can do that! So whatever choices you make, you have to live with the responsibility and consequence (*the result of <u>your</u> actions*). Even if you say that someone else made you do it (peer pressure); it was still <u>your</u> choice (<u>your</u> action). Well, enough said, I think you get it.

Now, let's talk about homework… If your parents tell you to do your homework when you first get home then do so. Even when they are not home, you should be doing it; that's being responsible. By the way, I like to suggest to parents to allow students time to relax or play (and have a snack) when they first get home from school so the brain can take a break. About a half hour or an hour later, you should pick a spot in the house or your room where you can study or do homework. Don't get distracted by watching TV or listening to the radio.

Some students say listening to music helps them do their work. If it does then that's ok. However, "disorderly" and extremely loud music can reduce your ability to recall what you studied. Instead, listen to music that stimulates your thinking (or your brain). On the other hand, watching TV is <u>never</u> going to help you get homework done. Sorry, but you cannot concentrate on the TV <u>and</u> your homework at the same time and expect to understand what you're doing.

The important thing about homework is to do it and turn it in. It's better to turn it in even if it's incomplete than not to turn it in at all because you're being responsible by turning it in. This doesn't mean you don't have to finish it; it means you do your best and complete what you understand. When you really don't understand and no one at home can help, you should turn it in <u>and</u> talk to your teacher about why it wasn't finished. Ask for help! This way you <u>are</u> being responsible.

So, let me get back to being a teenager… You <u>may</u> modify the way you dress, the style of clothes you wear, and change friends. Like it or not, your body will change, too; some of you will grow while others won't. This is all "normal"; a part of being a teenager. Sometimes you may freak out because you don't know what's happening to you (*or your body*) and maybe your parents haven't explained it to you. (*I'm talking about puberty, of course. Don't worry; we'll discuss it later in this chapter.*) Being a teenager should be groovy! You should be learning a lot (but *not just in school*). You should be spending time with family and friends; and you should be having FUN!

Just be yourself, be confident, and be who you are (*The Source Within*).

Sadly, middle school students can be hurtful at times by saying unkind words to others or by treating others badly just because they may wear different clothes, speak a different language, look differently than them, or because they don't seem as handsome or as pretty as someone else. This is what is considered bullying. It is <u>not</u> part of the *Source*. When you see or hear such things happen, you have to find *The Source Within*; you have to find the confidence to stand up for what is right. You need to know **every person is great just the way they are**. In other words, it is <u>not</u> ok to bully others; and it <u>is</u> ok to be different.

Now, let's turn our attention back to school... (*Sorry, but that's the teacher in me!*) School *is* one of the most important events of your young life, whether you are taught at home or at a public or private school.

Before you keep reading, tell me what you're willing to do to do well in school.

To succeed in school, **pay attention** in class and **do** your assignments. Learn the best way you know how. Just be aware some adults forget everyone learns at a different pace and in different ways. Be patient with your teachers and parents when they seem upset with you for not doing well or not understanding the lessons. Just be responsible and ask for help when you really don't get it! Oh yeah, be courteous when you ask for assistance because that's also part of responsibility.

Here are a few tips to help improve your middle school experience:

- ✓ Listen to your teachers and remember you are in school to learn.
- ✓ Pay attention to the lessons.
- ✓ Dress appropriately and be presentable.
- ✓ Be polite and respectful to everyone.
- ✓ Be on time to class with all of your needed materials.

✓ Ask your teacher to please explain it again when you don't understand. Depending on the teacher, you could either raise your hand from your desk or you could go up to his/her desk and ask for help during class. If that's difficult or embarrassing for you, ask after class.

✓ If the teacher doesn't respond to your plea for help, then ask your parents, an older sibling, or a friend to explain it. If you still don't understand, ask your parents if they could please write a note to your teacher explaining what you did not understand; or get a tutor.

✓ Always do your best.

✓ Get involved in after school activities where you can meet and make new friends (*and you're not home alone*).

✓ Don't copy someone else's work because yours may be correct while theirs is not.

✓ Create a study group with your friends.

✓ Don't do something just because everyone else seems to be doing it. (*You wouldn't jump off a cliff just because others jumped, would you?*)

✓ Be kind to others; if you don't seem to like them then just let them be. (*It's better to be a friend than to be a bully.*)

Let's link all of this to *The Source Within…* It is being responsible for your actions; it's also when you finally understand a concept because you paid attention and didn't quit. *The Source Within* does <u>not</u> ever, ever give up! It <u>is</u> determination. It's the courage to stand up for yourself in spite of what others say or think about you. It's also the part of you that studies, writes, listens, draws, plays an instrument, dances, sings, talks, and giggles!

Now, let's return to responsibility… It <u>is</u> actually kind of cool (*if you think about it*) because as you're growing up it becomes a part of your daily life. The more responsible you become, the more people will trust you. They see the *Source* active in you!

I think some parents, teachers, and other adults forget to teach you about responsibility. Yet, they expect it from you. This is where I think some parents (*and other adults*) go wrong with their teens; they expect you to be responsible without teaching you responsibility. Responsibility is something we have to learn. It seems the older we get, the more accountable we are held to it. Responsibility can be easy if you're taught about it early on, and that's why I am repeating it in this chapter.

It is part of *The Source Within*; the part that learns between "right" and "wrong". I mean, you don't have to be religious to know when you're doing something "wrong" or "right". You just know it; you feel it in your gut; and that's the intuition part. If we look at it from this point of view then life is all about learning! Learning is knowledge. Knowledge is power. Power is *The Source Within*!

By the way, friendships also have responsibility tagged to it. For example, if you're a true friend, you're always expected to tell the truth and to help a friend in need (*as long as it is not illegal or will not harm someone*). Friendships are sometimes tough in middle school because you can be influenced by others to think differently (even when it's not so nice). Like I said before, kids learn to be mean (either from parents, older siblings, friends, TV, or video games); you're <u>not</u> born mean. In middle school, the kicker is you're trying to "fit in" while striving to keep your friendships, which don't always work out. Loosing friends can be a hurtful experience, but if you rely on LOVE (*Source*) then you may get through it and <u>know</u> things (life) will be ok.

Believe it or not you will change friends like you change your clothes each day. No lie! This happens because some of you will want to be "popular". There's nothing wrong with that as long as you are sincere with your friends, and do <u>not</u> hurt them along the way. Believe it or not, only a few teenagers maintain their same friends from elementary school. What's not "right" is to hurt anyone in the process of <u>you</u> changing. Like I said previously, you may not like someone, but that doesn't mean you have to hate them. Find the *Source* (LOVE) and be kind.

Adolescence is also a "weird" time because your body is changing. In case you didn't already know, puberty is when your body's chemistry changes as well as your physical body. Your mood changes from one minute to the next; you can be happy one minute and sad, depressed, or angry the next. You can enjoy your family one day and not want to be around them the next. It's nuts! It can be scary, but it's "normal" (part of being a teenager). You just have to <u>realize</u> these changes are typical, <u>accept</u> them for what they are, <u>and ask</u> for help from your parents (*or a trusting adult*) when you don't understand what's happening to you and your body.

<u>Girls</u>, (oops, I mean young ladies) the "monthly cycle" will put your body through incredible changes and unless you understand exactly what is happening, you may get scared. Please ask your mom, an older sister, the school nurse, or an adult you trust to explain things to you. But please don't ask your friends because they're most likely going through it too and don't "get it" either.

Boys, (oops, I mean young men) you may notice some body changes too so don't think it's only the girls. For example, you will grow hair in interesting places and your voice will change (to kind of girly). The most important thing I can tell you is to please go to your father (or mom) and talk about it. If for some reason they prefer not to talk about it then go to an adult you trust. It is safer to ask an adult you trust than to ask a peer or friend because they're most likely going through it, too.

What can you do when your body starts to change?

Next, I'm going to provide a few tips for some of the things you may experience during puberty: (*Not all teenagers go through all of this at the same time or in the same way*) **(*REMEMBER THESE ARE JUST SUGGESTIONS NOT CURES!*)**

➢ acne (getting pimples)

Wash your face with mild soap and warm water and a clean washcloth; eat less or no chocolate or caffeine products.

➢ cramps (young ladies)

Do abdominal exercises; trust me, these help a lot! With your <u>parent's</u> <u>permission</u>, and if you need it, take some type of ibuprofen at home (at school, make sure you have a signed note from your parents; give the school nurse the medication with the note since in most schools you cannot take any kind of medication on your own); put a heating pad on your "tummy" (*not directly on the skin but over your clothes*); change yourself often and keep yourself clean. (*By the way, it's helpful to wear dark color pants during this time to avoid accidents; if you wear skirts, wear dark ones and shorts underneath.*)

➤ body odor

Ask your parents to please buy you body spray or deodorant with no aluminum. Try different brands until you find the one that works best to reduce the odor; bathe daily at home; wash your armpits and dry them before you put on deodorant or spray after PE class.

➤ sleepless or restless nights

Sometimes as your body is growing, you will want to sleep a lot more than usual; other times you may not sleep at all; sometimes you may have what they call a "wet dream" (this is an involuntary secretion of body fluids at night). This is typical and can happen any time; just be sure to talk to your parents or your doctor; go to sleep by 10 pm, Sunday through Thursday nights since you benefit from 8 hours of sleep; don't eat just before going to sleep; you may listen to relaxing music or Nature sound CDs to help you fall asleep.

➢ Body hair and other parts

Hair will grow in your "private" area, armpits, and legs; speak to your parents about the possibility of shaving (*but please, young men and young ladies, do <u>not</u> start shaving before you have to because it can cause skin irritation; or you could let it grow "natural" without shaving*); young men's voices may change to a higher pitch before it lowers so try not to be embarrassed; breasts may start to grow so young ladies ask your mom to take you to buy a bra and ask her how to know which ones are the best for good support.

Please, please, please speak with your parents about these changes. Like I said before, if your parents are not willing to talk about puberty (*your body changes or moods*) then find another trusting adult you could talk to.

The important thing to remember is turn to *The Source Within* for courage to face your middle school experiences, for the confidence to be yourself, for the determination to succeed in school, for the intuition to stay out of "bad" or dangerous situations, and for the LOVE to be reassured you are wonderful just the way you are!

Teens, email me if you have any comments or questions: source4peace@yahoo.com

CHAPTER 4

HIGH SCHOOL - NOW WHAT?

Congratulations and welcome to High School!

Let me be honest, though, going to 9th grade can be one of the toughest years you'll ever have as a teenager. I say this because you're most likely going to attend a new school, you'll be the "new" student and you will have no clue where anything is. Some Seniors (12th graders) will make fun of you and no one, not even your siblings, may talk to you because you're "fresh fish" (Freshman, 9th grader)! (*My brother didn't talk to me in the halls!*)

Well, once again, I say rely on *The Source Within* for the courage to face the challenges of high school (HS). Please remember this: **"It is none of my business what others think of me."** It means just what it says, and it will be one of the primary hardships you'll face. So be confident in who you are!

I suggest you find your confidence (*Source*), be smart, and plan ahead. For example, you could go visit the new HS before school begins by stopping by and asking for a tour. (I think most schools will do this if you ask.) You could also ask if they'll have a new student orientation. You may request a map of the school and highlight your classrooms, the cafeteria, library, gym, your counselor's office, and bathrooms. That way you won't be so lost the first days of school. Oh yeah, be careful who you ask for help because they're liable to send you to the wrong place! (*They're usually not being mean, but funny.*)

HS is challenging in many ways: you must become familiar with the school's layout, your siblings may not help you out at all, you may feel like you must dress like everyone else in order to fit in, your friends may not speak to you if they get together with a new group of "friends", your teachers will expect a lot more from you, your homework quantity will increase, your parents will expect you to be more responsible and mature (which may include watching younger siblings), there will be exams you must pass to graduate, and you may even have to find a job. These are just a few reasons why I said HS can be grueling.

If you have friends telling you they don't like you anymore, turn to *The Source Within* to gain the courage and confidence you will need to deal with the change. Keep LOVE in your heart so you don't hurt as bad or you're not mean to them. Remember, you are the only one that controls how you feel or react. <u>Know</u> you **are** LOVED. Be confident in yourself!

With the *Source* (LOVE), you're not going to be mean to others; use courage to be sincere in every situation (even when it hurts or it's difficult) and to be able to face each day. *The Source Within* is also your intuition. You know, the feeling you get in your gut when something just doesn't feel right. Well, that's *The Source Within* trying to keep you from harm. It could also be a way to help someone else stay out of a dangerous situation. Just be sure to follow "your gut" (intuition) whenever you feel it. *The Source Within* will guide you if you let it! It will not steer you wrong!

Life may be chaotic because your hormones are also raging! You may feel like you are loosing control of yourself, your emotions, and your sanity. This is typical for most teenagers in the world! <u>There's nothing wrong with you</u>; hormones change at various stages of life and these changes can cause chemical imbalances in our bodies. You're not loosing your mind or control over your emotions; it may be just a chemical imbalance. You can get through this tough time, too; you just have to <u>understand</u> what is happening

<u>and</u> <u>accept</u> it as a "normal" change of life. Once again, remember, you and only you control your actions.

You have a few options here:

❖ Read about puberty and chemical changes
❖ Ask the school nurse or your doctor for advice
❖ Ask to go to a therapist (counselor)
❖ Talk to your parents

(Please do <u>not</u> ask your friends because they'll say whatever they "know" or have heard about, and it's often wrong and doesn't help any of you.)

(Now, let's be clear; I'm talking about your body and <u>not</u> about being under the influence of some substance, like alcohol or drugs.)

Please tell your parents how you're feeling (scared, depressed, sad, confused, etc.); be as specific as you can, and ask them for advice or help. Whether you believe it or not, most parents do care and still LOVE <u>you</u>. Many parents just get caught up in their work or the younger kids so it seems like they don't care about you anymore. Believe me, most parents do care and want to help; you just have to speak with them. Whatever you do, **do <u>not</u> go through this time alone** because it can overwhelm you. As a result of feeling overwhelmed, many of you may harm yourselves, withdraw, or become involved with alcohol or drugs. This is **not** the answer and it is **not** the way to *The Source Within*. Instead, find LOVE, courage, and confidence (*which is all found within you*) to work through these awkward years.

Another stressful situation to deal with in HS is peer pressure. Most of the time, your "friends" (peers) will beg you to do things; when you say no, they pressure you until you give in or they shun you. When their requests feel wrong, return to your *Source Within*; find the confidence and courage to say no. Believe me this is not easy to do; I've been there, too. But you have to say __no__ when you feel something is wrong (rely on your intuition (*Source*)); leave, if you must. In spite of what you hear from your "friends" or see on TV shows or movies, you must stand up for yourself every time so others will know you're serious about not "going along" when you don't agree with it. A true friend and one that knows the *Source* would never put you in danger or harm you.

Let's move on to the next topic…Alcohol and drugs alter your ability to rationalize and think clearly. If you choose to ingest any of these unsuitable chemicals, you will certainly block the *Source*; you will slowly forget about it although it will **never, ever** leave you. These substances will alter your view of the world around you. For example, your grades will lower, as you "forget" to do your work; your attitude will change, as you increase use; you will become angry for "no reason at all", as you loose control of your emotions to the substance; you will say hurtful words to those who LOVE you, as the drugs stifle your feelings; you may partake in unsafe sexual behaviors, as your body's chemistry changes. I grew up watching some of my family do the things I just described, as drugs overpowered their lives. Not until they found *The Source Within* were they able to quit "using" and return their lives to a healthy and loving style.

To get through these difficulties, return to the LOVE (*Source*) within you. Remember, LOVE is sincere and does not harm you. (*I must clarify, the LOVE I am referring to is **not** "teenage love"; this LOVE is unconditional and has*

<u>nothing</u> to do with physical desires.) The *Source* is happiness, joyfulness, LOVE, honesty, trustworthiness, laughter, confidence, tears of joy, hugs, kisses, LIGHT, success, health, abundance, wealth, intelligence, clarity, etc.

The absence of LOVE is fear. Please understand LOVE and fear cannot coexist; it is <u>impossible</u> to hate and LOVE someone at the same time. Fear gives birth to hatred, and this does not solve conflicts. Wars do not solve conflicts. Look at world history and you'll see it has always been about power and greed, not about peace. Man has allowed his ego, pride, and selfishness to reign over others by force; man has used God as an excuse to kill; man created weapons, which has killed millions of innocent children; and all because of the absence of LOVE. Man lost his way to *The Source Within*; and thus, created destruction.

Anything not from the *Source* tends to generate fear, bias, racism, intolerance, injustice, hatred, war, injury, depression, inequality, fighting, pain, oppression, opposition, etc. These attributes come from a man (*or woman*) who does not have <u>and</u> does not know LOVE. And I would hope none of you would aspire to be that kind of man (*or woman*).

Notice I didn't include poverty or suffering because these are just conditions as a result of our own human actions. In addition, death is part of the cycle of life so it is not "negative" or "bad"; it is just another stage of our existence. I didn't include tears as "bad" because they release emotions. (*This is what I believe.*)

Another sensitive topic I wish to address is self-mutilation. Sadly, too many teenagers today are cutting themselves. Some believe it's happening because they're reading books that describe it. That may be so, but some teens do it because it tends to release "pain" associated with rejection, abuse, lack of LOVE from family, or lack of Self LOVE. The concern with this harmful act is the cutting can become more severe when you don't seek help. Sometimes, a friend could stop you from harming yourself and get help, but you must be the one to ask for the help otherwise you may keep doing it. Just remember that inflicting the pain will only release those "bad" feelings for a brief moment. Seek professional help to learn how to heal from the pain you feel.

Turn inward to find LOVE (*The Source Within*). Find the loving, beautiful Self you are. Rely on confidence to get you through those "bad" feelings. Pray (if you believe in prayer) to ask your god for strength and guidance to find a better way to deal with the "pain" (*and to send you someone who can help*). There is no shame in getting help and in telling someone you're hurting inside.

Now, let's lighten up the mood and talk about getting a job while in HS... First, apply for a job with flexible hours and which understands about school obligations. When you fill out the application for employment, be sure to complete the entire form. Do not lie on the application, as this could cost you the job. Dress appropriately for the interview (*depending on the position you're applying for, of course, depends on what you should wear*). By the way, a button-up shirt or blouse with slacks is always presentable; wear your pants at the waist, not sagging. Practice with your parents or a friend answering interview questions; this will help you relax. Arrive to the interview site at least 15 minutes prior to your meeting. Be courteous to everyone you meet at the place of employment. At times, the boss will ask the receptionist how you interacted with him or her. Once you have the job, arrive on time and dress accordingly.

<u>A suggestion</u>: put away a specific amount of money into a savings account each payday, pay your debts on time, and then buy things you need or want.

The last topic of this chapter is about your obligations at school… You need to pay attention in class and attend your classes; be on time; do the work assigned; in addition to your required courses, take classes you will enjoy (electives like Art or Shop); be sincere with teachers and staff; and excel by doing your best. By the way, studying, especially for State exams, will prove helpful. You could join extra-curricular activities; but make sure you can still meet your school, family, and job obligations and **don't stress by participating in too many**. It's also important to work with your school counselor each year to confirm you're taking the necessary courses to graduate, to obtain college information, and to find scholarship applications. <u>One last suggestion:</u> find a counselor, teacher, or staff member in HS who you can go to for help.

So, let's wrap it all up… To survive and succeed in HS, turn to *The Source Within*! Be confident in yourself; rely on courage to stand up for what you believe in; count on determination to follow your dreams even when others don't agree with them; use intuition to stay out of "bad" situations; and find LOVE to be who you are in spite of what others say or think of you.

Ok, High-schoolers! You may email me too if you wish, especially if you have questions about HS: <u>source4peace@</u> <u>yahoo.coom</u>.

Last chapter

There is Help

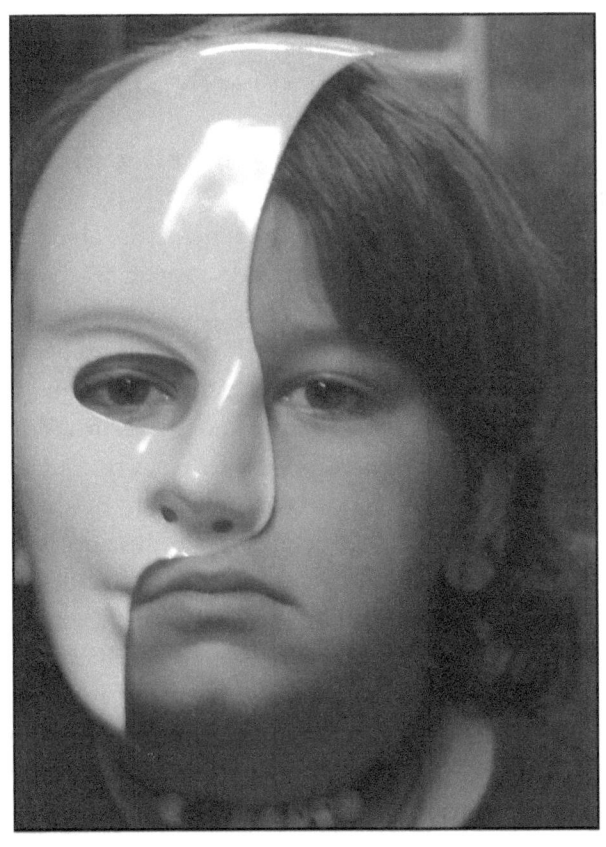

This last chapter will address abuse and neglect. Abuse is harmful to the human spirit and can make life seem impossible to live or get through. Another reason for writing this book was my desire to share some ways to deal with this issue. Abuse may be verbal, physical, emotional, psychological, or sexual; abuse could include bullies in school. Neglect is when a person fails to provide the basic human needs to another (food, shelter, clothing, <u>and</u> LOVE) or when one person completely ignores another (*for example, a parent who never, ever pays attention to their child*).

Abuse must be spoken about in order to stop it. Hiding or ignoring it does <u>not</u> solve it.

To solve it, I believe the person doing the abuse must be helped just as much as the person who was abused. Similarly, bullies in school need help. Most likely the abuser (or bully) was also abused, but that does **not** excuse their bad behavior. We could possibly help them to improve their behavior by showing them a way to find <u>their</u> *Source Within*. So you see, abuse affects everyone, and that's why counseling or some type of intervention is so important.

Choosing the "right" therapist (or counselor) is vital; this is a professional you talk to and who will guide you to find ways to help yourself and to deal with the situation. You'll know if he or she is the "right" one by following your "gut" feeling (intuition); that means if you feel comfortable talking to them the first time you meet, then he/she is probably a good person. But remember, you don't have to stay with a counselor who is not helping you, you don't feel comfortable with, or you don't trust. Do get help to heal from abuse or neglect you may have encountered or are experiencing now.

It's not easy to deal with abuse or neglect when it's done by someone you trust like family, friends, or peers. After the abuse or neglect happens, you may feel worthless, confused, not loved, and completely alone. But please remember there <u>are</u> people who LOVE you and who <u>can</u> help. It's crucial for you to seek help <u>and</u> find useful and safe techniques to survive it.

Writing, drawing, or some other activity may help. Some have used drawing as a way to "escape", and it helped them survive those tough times. Another activity you could do is writing; this can help you "let out" what you're feeling. Then, if you want to, you could share your writing with an adult you trust. You could also find activities to join after school to be in a safer environment, such as after-school clubs, sports, and the like. I am not saying doing any of these activities will solve the problem; I am saying they could help you get through it until you get help.

Other times, you may feel like there is something wrong with you or you did something to deserve the abuse. Do <u>not</u> <u>ever</u> believe that; those are all lies; **you did nothing wrong and you do <u>not</u> deserve to be hurt by those who are supposed to love you or by people you trust.** No one should ever, **ever** hurt you if they LOVE you. When someone loves you, they should not lie to you or harm you. If they love you, they will communicate LOVE and not cause you pain or harm.

So, if someone is abusing or neglecting you, find an adult you completely trust and tell them; as difficult as it may be, talk to your parents (as long as it's not one of them who is harming you). I know this can be scary and difficult, but you have to get someone to help you. Child abuse and neglect are against the law. You were born out of LOVE and deserve to be LOVED. Abuse and neglect are **not** LOVE.

But this is <u>not</u> a game or a joke. Do **not** make up stories about abuse if it did <u>not</u> really happen because you can ruin an innocent person's life.

If you are being abused or know anyone who is, call 1-800-4-A-CHILD (1-800-422-4453). It's a free call! Call Child Help anytime; there is someone to answer your call 24 hours a day, 7 days a week.

You may email me at <u>source4peace@yahoo.com</u>. Just be aware I'm required by law to report any abuse or neglect you share with me.

Let's summarize...

The Source Within is LOVE, confidence, courage, determination, intuition, and responsibility.

It is not about religion; it is about finding our Inner, Loving Self, and we are all born with it.

It is knowing you can do anything (confidence).

It's following your "gut" (intuition) to stay out of trouble.

It is never giving up, **ever** (determination)!

It is doing your part and being accountable for your actions (responsibility).

It is standing up for what you believe in and being yourself (courage).

Remember, only you control what you feel and how you react; and it is none of your business what others think of you.

The *Source* exists inside each one of us since birth; we just have to tap into this Power (Energy) to get through life's challenges.

Life is not "good" or "bad"; life just is. Life is whatever you make of it and how you "see" the experience. So make your life GREAT!

Dedication and Recognition

This book is dedicated to my mother and father (*May he rest in peace*); thank you for your unconditional love and support as I grew up. I'd also like to dedicate it to my Godchildren. This is also for all the students I have ever had the honor of teaching and to learn with. I hope this book continues to help you along your life's journey.

I'd like to thank my family and friends (too many to name individually) for their support and LOVE. A special thanks to my sister and my cousin-in-law for their input and editing of this book.

I am truly grateful to Author House for making this dream a reality so kids and teens around the globe (and their parents and teachers) may finally have a book to help them get through life's challenges.

Thank you, Spirit, for the clarity to know it was time to write this book and for the confidence to share this wisdom with children and teens; I am truly grateful.

[All photographs were released for printing with permission.]

About the Author

Zemí was born and raised in Puerto Rico; the fourth of six children. Her family moved to the United States when she was in 7th grade. Since she did not speak English and there weren't any language support services, she struggled in school. Many of the hurdles she faced are shared in this book. That's what inspired her to write it; she wanted to help kids and teenagers find ways to get through the tough times. To get through the hardships as she grew up and wishing to be successful, she relied on determination, confidence, responsibility, LOVE, and intuition (*The Source Within*).

Zemí is the pen name of Alécs Mojica; an ancestral name of Taíno Indians from her native Puerto Rico. She is an ordained Interfaith Minister and an Educator. Her intention is to promote peace and harmony through love by actively living in peace and sharing it with others, participating in interfaith dialogues, facilitating peace talks for kids and teens, and publishing.

For additional information, visit www.visionspath.com (click on Spiritual Choice link) or email: source4peace@yahoo.com.

Resources

Below are just a few websites and books I found that I thought you might find helpful. Check them out! Remember to ask your parents for permission before visiting any website.

http://www.kidinfo.com/School_Subjects.html
(Provides homework help in all subject areas)

http://www.kids.gov/
(K-8th grade information)

http://www.child.net/teenhelp.htm
(Lots of information about teen concerns)

(Book) Help Yourself for Your Teens: Real-life advice for Real-life Challenges by Dave Pelzer

(Book) The 7 habits of highly effective teens: the ultimate teenage success guide by Sean Covey

(Disclaimer: These particular websites and books are not necessarily supported or promoted by the author nor does the author approve any of their content. The author does not have any agreements or receive any monetary gain from listing them; they are merely resources thought to be of help.)

NOTES